AF270197

Dinosaur Graveyards in Asia

by Grace Hansen

Abdo Kids Jumbo is an Imprint of Abdo Kids
abdobooks.com

abdobooks.com

Published by Abdo Kids, a division of ABDO, P.O. Box 398166, Minneapolis, Minnesota 55439.
Copyright © 2022 by Abdo Consulting Group, Inc. International copyrights reserved in all countries.
No part of this book may be reproduced in any form without written permission from the publisher.
Abdo Kids Jumbo™ is a trademark and logo of Abdo Kids.

Printed in the United States of America, North Mankato, Minnesota.

102021

012022

Photo Credits: Alamy, Getty Images, iStock, Science Source, Shutterstock,
©Durbed p11 / CC BY-SA 3.0, ©Shutterstock PREMIER p.21

Production Contributors: Teddy Borth, Jennie Forsberg, Grace Hansen
Design Contributors: Candice Keimig, Pakou Moua

Library of Congress Control Number: 2021940126
Publisher's Cataloging-in-Publication Data

Names: Hansen, Grace, author.

Title: Dinosaur graveyards in Asia / by Grace Hansen

Description: Minneapolis, Minnesota : Abdo Kids, 2022 | Series: Dinosaur graveyards | Includes online
resources and index.

Identifiers: ISBN 9781098209452 (lib. bdg.) | ISBN 9781098260163 (ebook) | ISBN 9781098260514
(Read-to-Me ebook)

Subjects: LCSH: Dinosaurs--Juvenile literature. | Fossils--Juvenile literature. | Asia--Juvenile literature. |
Paleontology--Juvenile literature. | Paleontological excavations--Juvenile literature.

Classification: DDC 567--dc23

Table of Contents

Dinosaurs of Asia

Dinosaurs lived between 245 and 66 million years ago. After a dinosaur's death, its remains could turn to fossil if the conditions were right. This process takes more than 10,000 years!

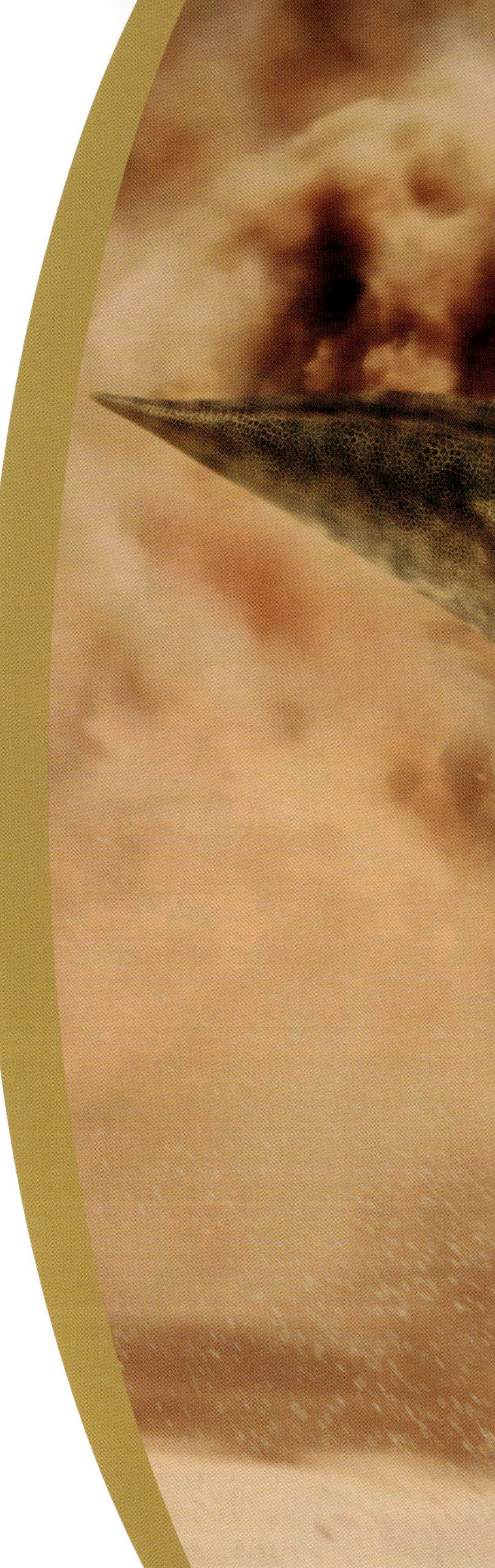

Every continent has dinosaur fossils, including Asia. Fossils are often found in **rock formations**. Some formations hold more remains than others!

Europe
Asia
Africa
N
W E
S

Shishugou Formation

The Shishugou Formation is in northwest China. It is known for its late Jurassic fossils. Remains of a large sauropod were discovered there.

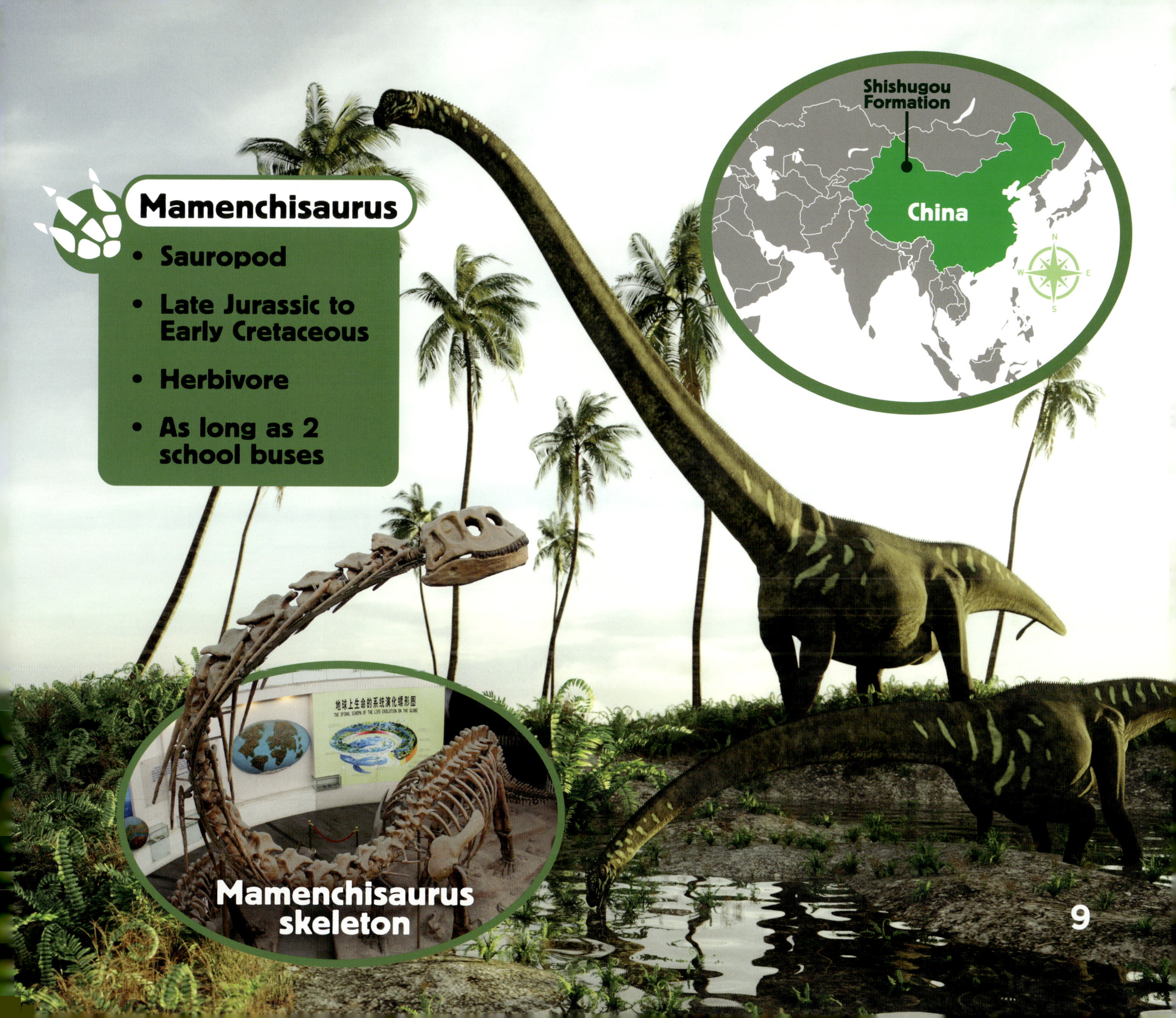

Mamenchisaurus

- **Sauropod**
- **Late Jurassic to Early Cretaceous**
- **Herbivore**
- **As long as 2 school buses**

Mamenchisaurus
skeleton

9

Theropods have also been
found there. The first remains
of Sinraptor were uncovered
in 1987. Years later, Guanlong
remains were discovered too.

Sinraptor
• Theropod
• Mid-to-Late Jurassic
• Carnivore
• Name means "Chinese plunderer"

Guanlong
• Theropod
• Late Jurassic
• Carnivore
• Known for unique crest on head

Djadochta Formation

The Djadochta Formation in Mongolia is special. There, the first confirmed **clutch** of dinosaur eggs was discovered. The eggs likely belonged to an Oviraptor.

Mongolia
Oviraptor
• Small theropod
• Late Cretaceous
• Omnivore
• Name means "Egg thief"
13

The first Protoceratops fossils were found in the formation. Other remains showed a fight with a Velociraptor! They likely died in a landslide.

Protoceratops
• Ceratopsian
• Late Cretaceous
• Herbivore
• The size of a sheep
Velociraptor
• Small theropod
• Late Cretaceous
• Carnivore
• Lots of sharp, pointed teeth
15

Kitadani Formation

Fukuiraptor is known from Japan's Kitadani Formation. It was probably the largest **predator** in the area at the time.

Fukuiraptor
Theropod
Early Cretaceous
Carnivore
As long as a Toyota Camry car
Japan

Udurchukan Formation

Olorotitan was hidden in a formation in far-east Russia until 1999. It grew to be 40 feet (12 meters) long! It also had a special head **crest** that flared out.

Russia
Udurchukan Formation
Olorotitan
Ornithopod
Late Cretaceous
Herbivore
Name means "Giant swan"
Olorotitan skull
19

Lameta Formation

The Lameta Formation is in central India. There have been many amazing fossil discoveries there!

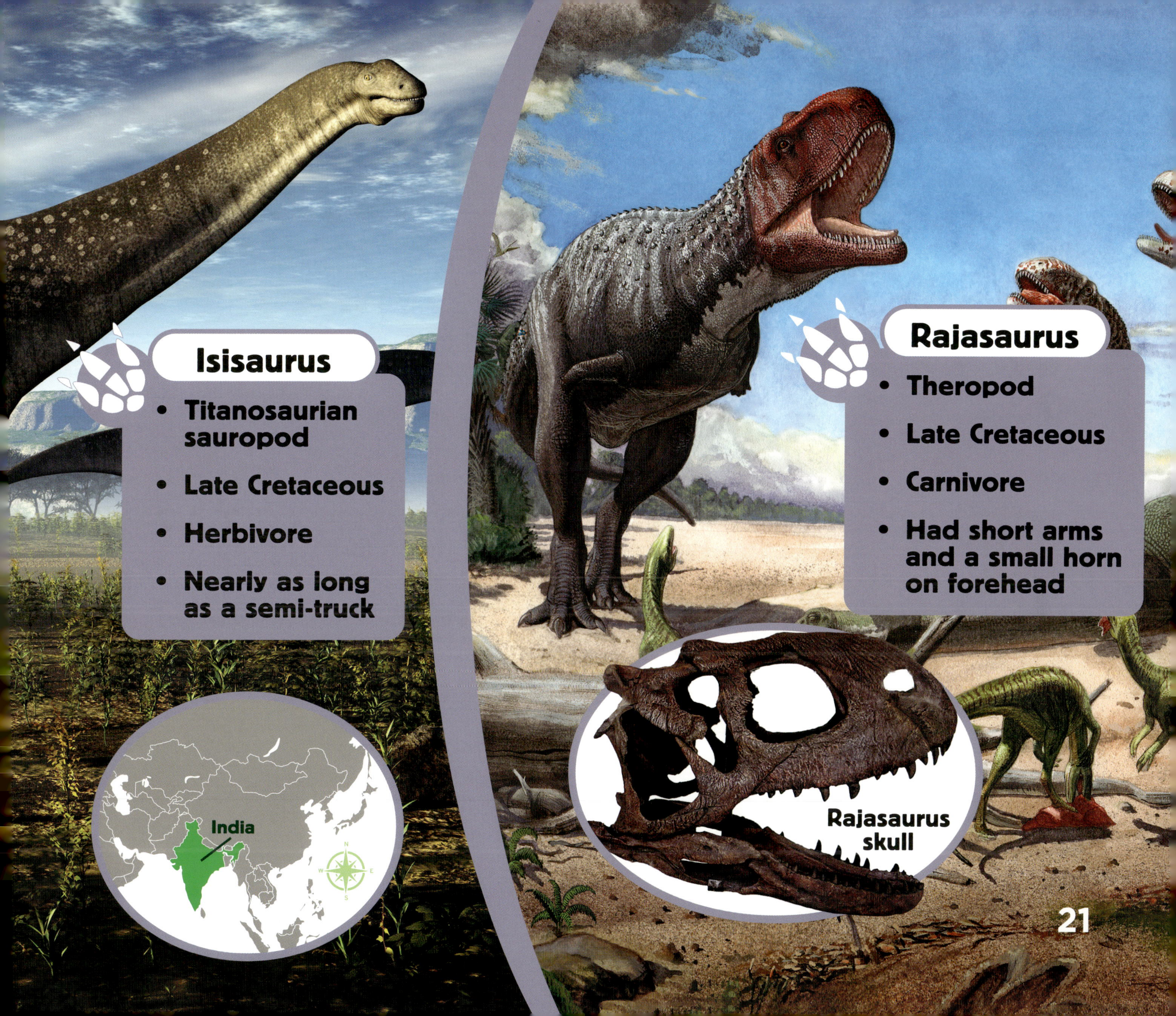

Isisaurus
• Titanosaurian sauropod
• Late Cretaceous
• Herbivore
• Nearly as long as a semi-truck
India
Rajasaurus
• Theropod
• Late Cretaceous
• Carnivore
• Had short arms and a small horn on forehead
Rajasaurus skull

Some Major Dinosaur Groups

Ankylosauria
- Four-legged
- Heavily armored
- Tank-like
- Some members had clubbed tails
- Herbivores

Ceratopsia
- Four-legged
- Solidly built
- Enormous skulls
- Long horns
- Sharp beaks
- Herbivores

Ornithischia

Ornithopoda
- Two-legged
- Beaked
- Had cheek teeth
- Herbivores

Stegosauria
- Four-legged
- Small heads
- Heavy, bony plates with sharp spikes down the backbone
- Herbivores

Sauropoda
- Four-legged
- Very large
- Long necks and tails
- Small heads
- Herbivores

Saurichia

Theropoda
- Two-legged
- From small and delicate to very large in size
- Small arms
- Carnivores and omnivores

Glossary

carnivore – an animal that eats other animals.

clutch – a nest of eggs.

crest – a tuft of feathers, bone, or fur on an animal's head.

herbivore – an animal that feeds only on plants.

omnivore – an animal that eats both plants and other animals.

predator – an animal that hunts other animals for food.

rock formation – a large body of rock that has a consistent set of physical characteristics that make it stand out from other bodies of rock nearby.

Index

Visit **abdokids.com** to access crafts, games, videos, and more!